Odes & Rhymes

Of Life & Times

Book 1

Alternative Advice On The Adult Adventure

By

AJ Brewster

Also by AJ Brewster

By Any Other Name (2012)

Published by AJ Brewster

This edition 2012

Any comments or queries regarding this book should be put to the author, AJ Brewster.

This page holds a poem that is dedicated to all my friends and family who have shown me so much support over the years with my writing and my website, www.thetwistedtalesofajbrewster.com. Thank you for all of your words of wisdom, encouragement, pick-me-ups and praise. Thank you for taking the time to read my stories and poems and being a shoulder of support when all around me seems to be going to the dogs. But most of all a big thank you to you all for being yourselves because if you hadn't of been you then I would never have been me.

To My Loved Ones

If one day you find I'm not there,
Do not cry, do not despair,
Just remember special times we've shared,
And remember just how much I've cared,
For you and all my friends it's true,
The love is deep for all of you,
And if you look within your heart,
You'll see we'll never be apart,
The memories that you hold so dear,
Will keep me alive for many a year.

Oh, and a big thank you to Lee Daly who designed the book's cover and has had put up with all my bad moods when I get writer's block, for which I am sorry and would just like to say I love you and I couldn't have done this without you.

☺

Contents

Section 1 – Provenance, Parentage, Puberty & Passing

Section 2 -.Love, Loyalty, Loneliness & Liberation

☺

Section 3 – Work, Wealth, Weariness & Whinging

Section 4 – Habits, Hobbies, Hoardings & Hankerings

Section 5 – Tragedies, Tyranny, Terrorism & Turmoil

Section 6 – Fears, Phobias, Freaks & Phantoms

☺

Provenance, Parentage, Puberty & Passing

☺

Life

Life is like a whirlwind,
Ever spinning,
Ever changing,
For the better,
For the worst,
Forever hoping,
Forever praying,
The best will come,
The worst will go,
Confusion is imminent,
Control is impossible,
Longing for freedom,
Longing for peace,
No problems,
No worries,
No doubts,
No fears,
Wishing,
Please all disappear,
Life is like a whirlwind,
Spiralling out of control,
Never stopping,
Always turning,
Until,
Existence evaporates,
Nothingness
End.

Inside My Teenage Mind

I hide in my room,
Won't let daylight in,
I live in the gloom,
Of my life's rubbish bin,
Junk food wrappers,
Litter my floor,
Countless dirty cups,
Teaming with spores.

I dress all in black,
And my body is thin,
Some say I look ill,
With my colourless skin,
Ignoring the world,
I'm permanently plugged in,
Listening to music,
That to others may sound grim.

My colour is black,
It matches my mood,
I don't talk that much,
Some say that I'm rude,
My response is a grunt,
Like Neanderthal Man,
I avoid conversation,
Wherever I can.

I don't like my parents,

I don't have many friends,

I was born to be alone,

I don't follow the trends,

I like to skip school,

Because I find it a bind,

There appears to be no logic,

Inside my teenage mind.

Mirrored Awareness

Is this a dream,
I'm sure I'm awake,
I'm staring in the mirror,
I can't believe what I'm seeing,
No longer the ugly girl of nightmares,
The shy girl who was teased and bullied at school,
No longer the fat caterpillar doomed to be cocooned in life's cruel world,
I look and I look,
The beauty is there once more,
Like a prisoner trying to escape,
It was always inside but now it shines out,
No longer hidden,
No longer locked up,
The light is free,
A light so bright,
So radiant,
It's still me in this mirror of mine,
Isn't it?
I am still here but I have blossomed,
I have grown,
I have changed,
Now I shine.

Go Out And Get It

It's about time you grew up,

Go face the world,

Stand on your feet,

Get out in the cold,

You're a big girl now,

Not easily led,

Time to prove yourself,

And get out of bed,

You know what you want,

Just go out and grab it,

Forget all the prejudice,

And sexist conflict,

Just do what you want,

Go enjoy what you do,

Because life is too short,

To sit there and rue.

Babies Are Not For Me

Babies, they're adorable,
Until one starts to cry,
If that happens I run a mile,
I really don't know why.

Can't deal with the dirty nappy,
Can't handle the sleepless nights,
How does a parent stay happy?
How do you make sure it's alright?

It's a life changing event,
That I really cannot see,
They say it's heaven sent,
But I'd rather it not be me.

A Father's Approval

A father's approval is a sort after thing,
They are very thin on the ground,
You spend all your life doing your best,
Trying to make your dad proud.

You work hard at school and earn yourself a B,
All he says is "Next time an A",
No word of encouragement, no "well done" from him,
It's no wonder you turned out this way.

All that you've had through all of your life,
Is criticism, comparisons and conflict,
Now your confidence is shattered and nothing else matters,
And you're wishing that he hadn't been so strict.

Nothing you've achieved was ever good enough,
No compliment would ever be given,
With only one direction you strive for perfection,
To a heart attack is where you've been driven.

Now the sad thing is that you're so far apart,
That to talk would just be a miracle,
And if you did achieve something that deserved your Father's praise,
Then the approval would be just satirical.

A Mother Like No Other

My mum is not like any other,
She's just not your typical mum,
She loves me just like a good mother,
But she encourages me to have fun.

She believes we should do what makes us happy,
And that we only learn from our mistakes,
When she gets drunk she talks about nappies,
And she's totally terrified of snakes.

She provides a shoulder to cry on,
She knows how to cook a good meal,
She knows what good pubs are worth trying,
To find a good pint of real ale.

My mum really likes a good rock tune,
ACDC is her favourite band,
Watching Angus on stage makes her swoon,
She is definitely their biggest fan.

From my mum I've learnt many a lesson,
She's brought me up to do the right thing,
We've had many a good drinking session,
Which ends up with some good debating.

I can say that I love my mum dearly,
She really stands out from the rest,
Even though she's not typical, clearly,
She's unquestionably the very best.

Life Is Just One Big Adventure

Life is just one big adventure,
Of that you can be sure,
You don't know where you'll ever end up,
Or what will knock at your door.

Take time to enjoy what you've got,
But remember to try something new,
The more you experience out of life,
The bigger the world is to you.

Life is just one big adventure,
You never know where it might go,
But I like to think, good or bad,
Whatever I learn helps me grow.

Never be scared to walk in the dark,
Never let fear hold you back,
Be individual stand out from the crowd,
Take life by the throat and attack.

Life is just one big adventure,
You may get lost on the way,
But I'd rather be lost and seeing new things,
Than have life stay the same every day.

Life has taught me one big thing,
Always look to the sun,
Smile, be happy, enjoy all you can,
Then the race of life will be won.

The Path Of Pressure

While growing up you tend to find,
That pressure dictates a way,
As everyone tries to control your life,
It presents a certain fray.

From the minute you're born into the world,
Your parents want you to talk,
And once you've said your very first word,
You're encouraged to get up and walk.

The next path is school where you're in competition,
With thirty children or more,
What used to be fun has now become a race,
To achieve the highest score.

Its then off to college and university,
There's not even time to yawn,
But your parents say that you need a career,
And a quarter of your life has gone.

University leads to a challenging job,
Where the competition is tough,
As everyone strives to get to the top,
You try to present the right stuff.

While following the path of your chosen career,
You're advised you need to settle down,
It's not as easy as it seems to find,
A love who will always be around.

You go out on dates meeting various people,
Trying not to get your heart broken,
Until eventually you find your one true love,
And those magical words are spoken.

You've barely finished your honeymoon,
When the parents start their coercion,
For it's now time to start a family,
And childcare becomes your exertion.

What used to grown-ups dictating your life,
Has been superseded by your child,
You've forgotten the joy that freedom did bring,
And can't remember the last time you smiled.

Childcare goes on for at least sixteen long years,
While it does you beg for retirement,
But you do get some joy by pressuring your child,
Now it's your job to be the pushy parent.

Old Age Comes To Us All

Retirement I'm told is when life begins,
When you truly enjoy your freedom,
So why do our children put us in homes,
And start to dismantle our kingdom.

They seem to think that once old age kicks in,
It's time to take control of our life,
No longer given the respect I deserve,
All they seem to give me is strife.

To them I seem doddery and old,
Unable to cope on my own,
When senility begins to set in,
They pack me up into a home.

As my wrinkles road map my wisdom,
I begin to think I know too much,
I'd share it but no one will listen,
They seem to think I've lost my touch.

Everyone shouts when they address me,
They think that my hearing is defective,
I always hear all that they're saying,
But my hearing it seems is '*selective*'.

I don't need advice from you youngsters,
When I need any help I'll just call,
Until then don't treat me like I'm five years old,
Remember old age comes to us all.

☺

Love, Loyalty, Loneliness & Liberation

The Optimistic Magpie

The optimistic magpie,
She lives on hopes and dreams,
Pinning her hope on happiness,
And dreaming about shiny things.

Distracting things in jeweller's windows,
They flash before her eye,
Always pining for that shiny ring,
The optimistic magpie.

She longs for something special,
She builds her nests to last,
Poor optimistic magpie,
Never learning from the past.

The optimistic magpie,
Her glass is always half full,
Flying through life in a daydream,
Her eyes hidden by the wool.

Hoping all her dreams will come true,
As she wakes up to another blue sky,
She sets herself up for another fall,
Poor optimistic magpie.

That Smile You Love

That smile you love,

You put it there,

How? You say,

By showing you care,

By giving me love,

By holding me close,

By telling me that,

You love me the most,

That smile you love,

It's all for you,

It's there because,

Your love is true,

A love that's shown,

In such special ways,

A love I know,

Will always stay,

That smile you love,

Lights up my face,

The beauty shines through,

Even the darkest place,

Your love shines through,

Like rays from the sun,

And I'll always smile,

Because you are the one.

Like Eleanor Rigby

Back in my house,

The loneliness creeps in,

Quiet as a mouse,

Then it's there,

I feel so alone,

Like Eleanor Rigby,

It doesn't feel like home,

When you're not with me,

A feeling that frightens me,

Dying alone,

With no one around me,

When will this feeling stop,

Everyone's there,

Friends and relations,

But nobody cares,

They just can't see it,

Hidden by a mask,

A beautiful smile,

Enduring the task,

Never showing my fear.

Windows To The Soul

Forgotten, let down,

Cheated, messed around,

Time to forgive, time to forget,

I can't seem to do it, my heart just won't let,

Into my shell, protected I hide,

I'm trying to trust but I'm staying inside,

Don't want to be hurt, I can see it again,

I'm trying to trust but how and when,

I want to believe, I want to be strong,

I know that you love me but tell me how long,

Will your mind change, will you think that it's best,

Will you find someone else and leave like the rest,

My dad always said if the truth be known,

Look in their eyes and true love will be shown,

The eyes are the windows to everyone's soul,

Look deep within them to determine their goal,

If you can see love deep in his eyes,

You'll know that it's true because love cannot lie,

So I guess that I am waiting for the first man I see,

Who's got beautiful eyes and true love for me.

Breaking Up Is Hard To Do

We need to talk,
Is what you said,
I knew it was coming,
I wished I were dead.

It's not going to work,
Can you not see,
This relationship is doomed,
It's not your fault, it's me.

No there's nobody else,
I just want to be alone,
I need my own space,
My own place, my own home.

I've heard it all before,
The excuses and the lies,
What makes you think I can't see,
Through your stupid disguise.

I'm not naïve,
I know there's another,
I know that you're lying,
I know it's a cover.

Just tell me the truth,
Don't treat me this way,
I deserve so much better,
So bugger off, leave today.

Loving You

How could it be that this feelings so strong,
I feel that together is where we belong,
But it's been such a short while so how do I know,
That a love so deep and strong will grow.

Thinking back to the day we met,
A day in my life I will never forget,
Your smile so sweet and eyes so bright,
A love so deep, so true, so right.

Never in my life have I met such a man,
Who takes my breath away like you can,
Whose kisses can make all time stand still,
Whose love helps me climb all of life's hills.

A smile that could melt anyone's heart,
I fell deep in love right from the start,
From the very first smile, the very first glance,
I knew in an instant to take the chance.

When I look in your eyes so beautifully blue,
I can see your love, a love so true,
It feels like I'm under some kind of spell,
And I know that you're feeling the same way as well.

A passion so deep, a love so pure,
Never in love have I been so sure,
I long to be with you every day,
And by your side I promise I'll stay.

To love and to cherish and never to part,
My love for you comes straight from the heart,
I'll love you always and leave you never,
Please say you'll be mine forever and ever.

Smile

As I walk through life alone,
So many friends but no one's at home,
I continue to smile despite feeling sad,
Always replying, "I'm not too bad".

A friend will ring to talk of woe,
I listen and then it's time to go,
Listening because it's my greatest skill,
Of other's problems with life's steep hill.

No one hears my silent plea,
No one ever listens to me,
Some days all I can do is cry,
But I smile the smile of a well-practiced lie.

No one rings to ask if I'm good,
I get the feeling that no one would,
So long as everyone else is fine,
I'll struggle along with this life of mine.

As I walk through life alone,
So many friends but no one's at home,
And as I sink into deep depression,
I smile just to give a good impression.

Liberation

Your way or the highway there was no compromise,
From the minute we met I was taken in by your lies,
Those rose-tinted glasses were misleading my eyes,
A selfish individual in a loving disguise.

If I'd have known back then what I clearly know now,
I'd have left you to rot with that silly old cow,
Would never have agreed to a marital vow,
It's amazing just how much you wouldn't allow.

For eight arduous years I was under your thumb,
Spending time wondering what the hell I had done,
Liberation showed me I was just being dumb,
And that I'm better off without you in the long run.

The moment I was free from your officious grip,
I could see that we were always joined at the hip,
Once I'd got away from your belittling lip,
I decided to take a spontaneous trip.

It was then that I realised I didn't need you,
And that everything you'd told me just wasn't true,
Your presence just made me feel irrelevant and blue,
So I gladly see you off with an overdue adieu.

Now that you're gone I can live life as I want,
Away from all of your disparaging taunts,
Floating through life with a hint of a flaunt,
Enjoying the life of a free debutante.

Our Future In Racing

Together forever,

Growing wrinkly and old,

Racing Motobility scooters,

Up and down the road.

We'll have one each,

And we'll ride with vengeance,

Tormenting the kids,

And taking no nonsense.

We'll ride round the shops,

Blocking the aisles,

Knocking down displays,

While discussing our piles.

We'll ride down to the pond,

To feed all the ducks,

We'll live life to the full

Because we don't give a hoot.

Just enjoying our time,

Every minute together,

Growing old and wrinkly,

Together, forever.

I'm In Love With A Punk Rock Guitarist

I'm in love with a punk rock guitarist,
It's a really funny affair,
My parents just can't seem to get round,
His red, white and blue spiky hair.

I'm in love with a punk rock guitarist,
He's talented on the guitar,
His music is truly amazing,
And I'm sure that he'll make a good star.

I'm in love with a punk rock guitarist,
He's talented, clever and fit,
And as he plays at the Greyhound,
I know that he'll be a big hit.

☺

☺

Work, Wealth, Weariness & Whinging

Rat Race

Joining in the rat race,
To earn an honest keep,
There's not much left come pay day,
'Coz bills they aren't that cheap,
You join the queue of traffic,
The proverbial 'Employed Sheep',
Doing such a mundane job,
All work, no play then sleep.

Joining in the rat race,
Queuing in your car,
You're told of great promotions,
You dream that you'll go far,
Instead you sit there from nine to five,
Your mind turning to tar,
Believing that as time ticks by,
You'll escape to Shangri-La.

Joining in the rat race,
You feel you're doing time,
It's like a bloody penance and,
You've done no bloody crime,
If anyone should be locked up,
It's the Government of this time,
For stealing all our hard earned cash,
And thinking that it's fine.

Joining in the rat race,
I hope it's not in vain,
If I save my pennies hard enough,
And If I can stay sane,
One day I'll fulfil all my dreams,
One day I'll break this chain,
Then maybe I can enjoy life,
Claim my freedom back again.

Money

Money, no matter how much I earn,

Spend, spend, spend, I never learn,

Try as I might I cannot save,

When it comes to cash I cannot behave,

It slips through my fingers like grains of sand,

I've got nothing to show for it in my hand,

It doesn't come easily but it sure as hell goes,

Whatever it's spent on nobody knows.

Poo's At Work

I love to do my poo's at work,
It saves my toilet paper,
And the pleasurable thing about it is,
I'm paid while I'm on the crapper.

Writer's Block

Caught in a quagmire,

Something to inspire,

An idea to bloom,

I want it real soon,

I'm stuck in a pit,

Feeling like shit,

I sit with my block,

Staring at the clock,

Come on good ideas,

I'm so close to tears,

I'm stuck at the station,

It's like constipation,

Why can I not write,

Inside I just fight,

For ideas to flow,

So I can let go.

Enough Of It All

The 'romance box' is empty,
The 'passion bucket' has a hole,
The 'stress chest's' blown capacity,
I'm fed up of it all.

The boss is hanging on my back,
The kids have too much cheek,
The shit has hit the proverbial fan,
And it's starting to bloody reek.

The dog is chewing the furniture,
The cat keeps being sick,
I'm beginning to think it'll never end,
And it's getting on my wick.

I can't remember the last time,
I relaxed and had a ball,
I could really do with a few days off,
Because I've had enough of it all.

Benefit Fraudsters

Benefit Fraudsters seem to think they can live above the law,
By claiming they are out of work and pretending to be poor,
While all the time they are working being paid cash in hand,
How do they get away with it I really don't understand?

They're skilled at completing forms and know exactly how to claim,
And when confronted they make out they aren't the ones to blame,
They are quick to make excuses claiming that they didn't know,
Pleading ignorance but it's clear they aren't as pure as driven snow.

Benefit Fraudsters get my goat but what really makes me cross,
While I am working my butt off the idle skivers doss,
Living on my hard earned cash taxed from my monthly wage,
Enjoying their free holiday while I contain my rage.

They keep producing kids like they're on a factory line,
So they can claim more money to live their life of crime,
And while I juggle my finance trying to balance my accounts,
These families with no values enjoy a life of free hand-outs.

Me And My Clone

If only I could clone myself,
I live one life with two,
The clone could got to work for me,
And they wouldn't have a clue.

I lay in bed in the morning,
Ignoring the alarm,
I'd spend the days just having fun,
What could be the harm?

I'd get done all I wanted to do,
Work wouldn't stand in the way,
The clone would earn my money,
While I could spend and play.

If only I could clone myself,
I know it's just a dream,
But imagine the possibilities,
They're endless it would seem.

Work Life

With a blink of an eye the weekend has past,
And all my holidays appear to go just as fast,
It seems like the work life is never ending,
With its constant stress and boring ear-bending.

Work life and boredom go hand in hand,
As time trickles by like the hourglass sand,
I try to look busy and show an interest in my job,
With the pittance I'm on I feel like I'm robbed.

When finally its home time I'm tired and weary,
I can't have any fun because I just feel dreary.
All I want to do is go sleep in my bed,
But I know when I wake up I'll want to be dead.

As the sun determines a new day dawning
And my mouth just can't seem to stop all the yawning,
The alarm triggers off a fear in my head,
It's only bloody Tuesday and I've got to get out of bed.

I drag myself in for another monotonous day,
Wishing it was Friday so I would nearly be away,
With the long afternoon dawns a gloomy realisation,
There's still three more days before the train leaves the station.

Still three more days before I can relax,
Working my butt of just to pay tax,
Earning my money to have my pay day,
Just so I can enjoy a weekend of play.

If I Won The Lottery

If I won the lottery,
This is what I'd do,
I'd like to help some animals,
By donating to a Zoo.

If I won the lottery,
I'd make sure my family's set,
So they wouldn't have to worry,
About incurring any debt.

If I won the lottery,
I'd pay off all my loans,
Then I'd set about investing in,
A house that I could own.

If I won the lottery,
I'd become a volunteer,
I'd give up working nine to five,
To bring pensioners some cheer.

If I won the lottery,
I'd give my friends a treat,
And buy my man his favourite guitar,
Because he makes my life complete.

But if you win the lottery,
Please try to think of me,
The poor unpublished poet,
Merci mon cher ami.

Boredom

Boredom sets in,
Life withers away,
I just can't be bothered,
To get up and play.

The clock ticks the seconds,
I watch the hands go round
Minute by minute,
Aware of the sound.

My brain starts to slow,
The world blurs around me,
My mind starts to go,
I start to feel sleepy.

Am I awake or asleep?
Am I dead or alive?
Can't carry on like this,
Need stimulation to survive.

My eyelids get heavy,
I start slumping in my chair,
Is the bloody clock working?
It just isn't fair.

The minute hand is frozen,
I'm sure that it's stopped,
Every time that I look,
At that bloody dead clock.

I want to go home,
Do something more exciting,
Than sit here so bored,
With the sleep that I'm fighting.

At times I could swear,
That the clock's in reverse,
That it's cheating me of time,
Making me feel worse.

Sometime I think,
I could die of this boredom,
As I sit here wishing,
For home time to come.

☺

Habits, Hobbies, Hoardings & Hankerings

A Chocolate Fix

When I'm in need of a chocolate fix,
I'll start it off with a King Size Twix,
I'll turn to Bounty when in need of the tropics,
For a hazelnut in every bite it's got to be Topic.

While having a Star Wars movie day,
It can only be a Galaxy far, far away,
It's Milky Bar while wearing my ten gallon hat,
And when on a break it can only be KitKat.

While dancing I partake in a Cadbury's Twirl,
Or sometime I go for a Hazelnut Whirl,
But there's only one chocolate that gives me a rush,
And that's Hotel Chocolat for when I'm feeling flush.

Wannabe Welly Wearers

Designer Wellingtons and Range Rovers,
'Must Have' Tepee Tents,
Two point five children,
Headlining 50 Cent,
The Wannabe Welly Wearers,
Enter the festival gates,
Change into their hemp shirts,
And meet up with their mates,
They stand around smoking pot,
While talking above the acts,
Drinking designer cider,
While their kids hang out in packs,
They forget that they are parents,
While they take their 'special trip',
Eating tofu burgers,
While pretending their young and hip,
For one weekend they leave their lives,
And mix with the 'lower' class,
If only they were invisible because,
They're a right pain in the arse,
They have no idea who the small bands are,
They don't even give them a chance,
They're just here to see the headliners,
And get high in the tent of trance,
For one weekend they're hippies,
At one with Mother Earth,
When really they're just hypocrites,
With no *real* eco-worth.

Expiration From Smoke Inhalation

Expiration from smoke inhalation,
Lungs destroyed by disease,
The pain goes on for far too long,
With drugs you try to ease,
You never listened to doctors,
Or to the friends that cared,
You never thought, 'hey let's give it up',
So the heartache could be spared.

The Cancer crept around your body,
Slowly killing you from inside,
As your breathing got much harder,
The Cancer enjoyed a free ride.
All your friends are watching you now,
As you make your final journey,
An ironic end to a smoker's life,
When the cremation starts it's burning.

Fad Diet Bimbo

Fad Diet Bimbo,
She's skinny and she's neat,
She complains that she's fat,
Even though her size is petite.

She's on a different diet,
From one week to the next,
Always talking about eating,
Because her mind is not complex.

She reads Cosmopolitan,
Hello and Heat,
Looking for advice,
From another eating cheat.

She drives you insane,
With her constant diet chatter,
You wish she'd put a cake in it,
Because at least then she'd be fatter.

She'll only be happy,
When she's a size zero,
A skeleton with skin,
And nowhere left to go.

She's a Fad Diet Bimbo,
She believes she is too fat,
She'll bore you to tears,
With her constant fat chat.

Possessions

Designer named trainers,
A big flashy car,
None of these things,
Make you who you are.

They're only items,
They're only possessions,
Keep up with the Jones',
Is your great obsession.

They don't make you happy,
They only keep you poor,
You spend all your money,
And still you want more.

With all the money gone,
You put them on your card,
You end up in debt,
And life becomes real hard.

You haven't learnt your lesson,
You're completely unreal,
You need more possessions,
You then decide to steal.

You end up in prison,
In trouble with the law,
Because you won't be yourself,
And you always want more.

Three Thirty-three In The Morning

It's three thirty-three,
And I'm dying for a wee,
I really want to sleep,
But it just won't keep,
I want to stay a dreaming,
But my bladder is a screaming,
Why can't it leave me be,
Until the alarm awakens me,
There's nothing more annoying than the early morning pee.

You Booze, You Lose

Inebriated,

Can't remember your name,

You're the king of comedy,

In your drunken fame,

You'll laugh at yourself,

While they all laugh at you,

You drink so much beer,

That tomorrow you will spew,

But for the time being,

You'll forget about that,

By dancing and drinking,

And acting a twat,

You'll forget the hangover,

Put off the pain,

And keep with the drinking,

'Til it's morning again.

Procrastination

Procrastination,

My favourite pastime,

Life's best diversion,

Served best with wine,

A chocolate or two,

Placed on the side,

A lifetime could pass,

When you jump on this ride.

The Battle Of The Bulges

It’s time for the Battle of the Bulges,
As I take on the fight of the fat,
I need to forget about indulges,
And take notice of what I pick at.

No sweets, treats or unnecessary snacking,
But it’s hard to stick to this regime,
It’s self-discipline that I’m lacking,
As I fight with the tub of ice-cream.

I’m counting my calories just like sheep,
As I try to cut down my carbs,
My craving materialize in my sleep,
As I dream about a Tarte au Rhubarbe.

I started my diet today,
So I my forget the sweet indulges,
I must avoid fat come what may,
As I fight the Battle of the Bulges.

Sweet Cravings

I can hear you calling me,
From the fridge in which I left you,
I can hear you taunting me,
Into going to collect you,
I try to forget you're there,
As my urge becomes much stronger,
It's more than I can bear,
Can't fight the need for much longer,
I try to keep myself busy,
Hoping the cravings will subside,
I start to feel quite dizzy,
As they remain unsatisfied,
The obsession takes control,
Of my desire to be fulfilled,
Like a puppet I do stroll,
Uncontrollably weak willed,
As I anticipate my prize,
I begin to salivate,
But I cannot believe my eyes,
When met with an empty plate,
How could I be so deluded,
Thinking it would still be there,
My craving has been precluded,
Pudding thief you'd better beware.

☺

Tragedies, Tyranny, Terrorism & Turmoil

News Today (Distraction Of The Blind)

Have you read the news today,
Do you read all it's got to say,
Or do you find yourself drawn away,
By the tabloid's diversionary sway.

Page one describes the plight,
Of the footballers one night,
Of extramarital delight,
On his international flight.

While hidden in the pages,
Are the government's real wages,
And the secret votes it stages,
On the NHS cut changes.

While reading about expenses,
There's a cut in our defences,
With the government pretences,
Will we ever see our senses.

Politicians hide their lies,
With another fuel price rise,
Tragedy turns to disguise,
As a princess sadly dies.

If you read between the lines,
There is something you might find,
The news that hidden behind,
The 'distraction of the blind'.

Haribo Gangster

Just out of nappies,
He's still mummy's boy,
Haribo Gangster,
Has found his new toy,
Vengeance is his,
With his knife or his gun,
And when he's finished,
He goes home to mum,
He sits down to dinner,
With his smug attitude,
Haribo Gangster,
Thinks it's cool to be rude,
He hangs on street corners,
With all of his friends,
Picking on people,
Who cannot defend,
Themselves from his torment,
They're frightened you see,
Coz Haribo Gangster,
Is as hard as can be.

Global Disaster

NB: written to the tune "A Few Of My Favourite Things"

Concrete and tarmac
Steel and glass buildings
Tesco and Asda,
With smooth metal railings,
Five storey car parks dotted here and there,
Global disaster you'd better beware.

Carbon emissions,
Empty public transport,
Road rage and traffic jams,
And rising crude import,
Pile ups on motorways causing delay,
Global disaster is coming your way.

Killing off habitats,
Destroying the food chain,
Clearing the rain forests,
Causing more acid rain,
Extinction is imminent there's nothing we can do,
Global disaster is coming for you.

When the bees die,
When the birds fly,
When the crops all decline,
Will we remember to respect the Earth,
Or will we think that we'll be fine.

Terrorist On Terra-Firma

Terrorist on terra-firma,
What a lovely guy,
Prepared to die for his religion,
On land or sea or sky.

Terrorist on terra-firma,
He's a hero in his town,
Take your slaughterers views elsewhere,
Along with your dynamite crown.

Terrorist on terra-firma,
Immigrant indeed,
Sponging of our government,
To make your bombs with speed.

Terrorist on terra-firma,
Camouflaged by kindness,
We show you hospitality,
You bomb us for our blindness.

Terrorist on terra-firma,
He's admired back at home,
You don't belong in our country,
Go back where you belong.

Terrorist on terra-firma,
You're not welcome in our land,
Your religion doesn't make any sense,
It should be bloody banned.

Brainwashed Heroes

Sugar-coated posters draw you in,
Careers to last a lifetime,
Seeing the world and getting paid,
Just sign on the dotted line,
A world where villains are defeated,
And the heroes always win,
In the land of hope and glory,
This Disneyland of dreams.

The President's not happy,
They aren't doing things his way,
It's time to show them boys,
He doesn't care what they say,
The orders are sent out,
Grab your guns boys its war,
Everyone's so brainwashed,
The reason why is unsure.

Time is of the essence,
Kill them before they kill you,
Don't worry lads we'll let you know,
When spilling blood is through,
We'll send you your home comforts,
It'll be just like a holiday,
Just get the evil bastards and,
Remember you're on pay.

You think you are invincible,
A hero through and through,
But that's just what the other guys thinks,
When he aims his gun at you
Your family start to worry,
As casualties start to rise,
But still they vote the same guy in,
While innocent people die.

Times They Are A Changing

He used to be a jukebox hero,
He had the stars in his eyes,
Now he's just an Xbox zero,
Who crashes, burns and dies.

The times they are a changing,
What we used to know is gone,
There's been some re-arranging,
Virtual Living is how it's done.

No longer do we go out on dates,
We find true love online,
Through social networks we chat with our mates,
Because no one has the time.

We have lost the art of conversation,
The board game has died a death,
Instead we're farming digital plantations,
Growing fantasy baby's breath.

As avatars we live out our lives,
Never having to leave the house,
Getting shopping delivered to our drives,
By ordering it with our mouse.

We don't know how to live for real,
We've forgotten what's outside,
It's time we grabbed life's steering wheel,
To experience the 'real life' ride.

DJ Dictators

They're not quite as bad as Gadaffi,
Or as evil as Saddam Hussein,
But when it comes to ruling our airwaves,
Radio DJ's dictate just the same.

They only play top 40 records,
Which they repeat on a regular basis,
You find yourself unintentionally singing,
As you go into a brain numbing stasis.

Since XFactor's TV debut,
You don't even need originality,
The charts have turned to karaoke,
And the music has become criminality.

Unless you're a big record label,
DJ's don't even care how you feel,
They never promote any interesting bands,
Oh how music misses you John Peel.

Parliament's Infinite Wisdom

Trouble erupts in our cities,
As protestors get out of hand,
Parliament gathers committees,
While police try to take command,
The protest has lost its direction,
As peace explodes into a riot,
Chaos spreads like an infection,
Even kids want to join in and try it,
Businesses and homes are destroyed,
By cowards who hide behind masks,
The riot police are deployed,
But are overwhelmed by the task,
The rest of the country is raged,
As innocent people are hurt,
While looters go on the rampage,
The police force is on red alert,
As our cities are glowing with fire,
Parliament goes into debate,
The countries leading men conspire,
Deciding the police force's fate,
Parliament in its infinite wisdom,
Decide that it's time for cut backs,
And police receive this time bomb,
While rioters continue their attacks.

Mother Nature

It's time for you to listen and to heed the warning signs,
Mother Nature has a voice and don't think she'll be kind.
For every forest habitat destroyed because of greed,
Prepare for a reprisal from a harsh mistress indeed.
She's not a woman to mess with so don't think she's meek or mild,
Her only aim is to protect the Earth and everything that's wild.
Disruption by an ash cloud or perhaps some heavy rain,
Some may not heed her warnings and her pleas may be in vain.
She'll then get more destructive while you're busy playing war,
An earthquake and a tidal wave should make you notice more.
So think before you drop that bomb or put in another road,
Mother Nature owns the Earth so you'd do well to leave alone.

Christmas Comes Earlier Each Year

I used to really love Christmas,
The turkey, the presents and the cheer,
But now that I'm older I dread it,
Coz Christmas comes earlier each year.

You barely get through the summer,
When shops put out new 'seasonal' stock,
It's just the first week in September,
And you're expected to hang up your sock.

For the next three months you're bombarded,
With silly Christmas adverts and songs,
Are the salesmen completely retarded,
To deliver this hype for so long.

I'd like to go back to my childhood,
When Christmas was magically near,
A time when you didn't lose excitement,
Coz Christmas comes earlier each year.

☺

☺

Fears, Phobias, Freaks & Phantoms

Halloween

Jack-o-Lanterns, trick or treat,
Ghosts and devils walk the street,
Kids dressed up as horror stars,
With witches hats and fake scars,
Apple bobbing, pumpkin heads,
Rubber spiders in fake webs,
Skeletons that glow in the dark,
Werewolves playing in the park,
Vampires complete with capes and bats,
Witches with brooms and black cats,
Michael Myers is on TV,
This is what Halloween means to me.

Hammer Horror Rules

The Hammer Horror's movie debut,
Was in 1955,
With The Quatermass Xperiment,
Bringing movie horror to life.

Next came The Curse of Frankenstein,
Starring Peter Cushing and Christopher Lee,
They became my favourite actors,
True icons throughout Hammer's history.

Then came the rebirth of Dracula,
With Lee's scary bloodshot eyes,
Cushing took the Van Helsing role,
And saw to Lee's demise.

Not born when they first came out,
I used to watch them on TV,
Huddled up in a blanket,
Nothing would ever scare me.

The Curse of the Werewolf and The Devil Rides Out,
Quatermass and the Pit,
Historically inspired Countess Dracula,
Brought to life by Ingrid Pitt.

The movie production died a death,
When funding became very low,
So they took their talents elsewhere,
And produced a TV show.

The Hammer House of Horror,
Was a creepy TV show,
With twists and turns and jumpy bits,
You couldn't guess where it would go.

Then Gothic Horror appeal returned,
And movie reels began to spool,
Hammer has truly risen from the grave,
Because Hammer Horror Rules.

My Life As A So Called Ghost

I'd like to introduce to you,
My life as a so called ghost,
I'm vaguely here to some,
But invisible to most.

It's true I can blend into any crowd,
Too translucent to be seen,
The only people who see me around,
Are the ones who need something.

Whether sitting in the office,
Or walking round the shops,
I go about my business,
And no one ever stops.

No one says, 'Why thank you',
Or 'You've done a real good job',
No one says, 'Let me do that',
It really makes me sob.

It may seem just like magic,
Or like a poltergeist,
The jobs all get completed,
But they assume it's just the mice.

No one notice if I'm here,
No one's bothered if I'm not,
No one worries if I'm happy,
No one cares if I lose the plot.

Always taken for granted,
And shown no appreciation,
My humour starting to suffer,
From a grave depreciation.

I'm starting to think I'm not alive,
You won't believe it's true,
But when I do eventually die,
I'm coming to haunt you.

So with that I'd like to conclude,
My life as a so called ghost,
I'm vaguely here to some,
But still invisible to most.

Dreams Of Pigs With Angels Wings

Dreams contain the strangest things,
Like flying pigs with angel wings,
Stripy socks,
Tick tock clocks,
Fields as gold as wedding rings.

Cats with smiles and little boots,
Trains that pass with hooty toots,
Lollipop trees,
Birds and bees,
Frogs that dance with bright red lutes.

Loads of cars like Wacky Races,
Evil clowns with trouser braces,
Seas of blue,
Tea for two,
Gangsters holding violin cases.

Black beard pirates drinking rum,
Dogs that chase and bite your bum,
Scraggy valleys,
Dark damp alleys,
Mysterious shadows that make you numb.

Teddy bears with pointy teeth,
Tall dark trees without a leaf,
Killer dolls,
Moaning souls,
Sharks that swim within the reef.

Zombies, ghouls and vampire bats,
Scary men with pointy hats,
Puddles of mud,
Rivers of blood,
Cold, wet cellars infected with rats.

Fast you run, it must not catch you,
The sea is black, no longer bright blue,
Darkness falls,
Evils Calls,
Run and hide before it gets through.
WAKE UP!!!

Werewolf

I feel the change,
The moon is right,
So round and full,
It's coming tonight.
I feel an urge,
To hunt and kill,
It's not like me,
It's not my will.
I feel the monster,
Growing inside,
The moon is full,
I cannot hide.
My body is aching,
My fingers stretch,
My chest is changing,
I start to wretch.
I scream in agony,
I cry with pain,
I shout, 'Oh no',
'Not this again'.
As my body changes,
A hunger breeds,
Craving raw flesh,
To fulfil my needs.
Beware all those,
Who wander the night,
You may become,
My next meal tonight.

The Spider called Fred

See the spider, I call him Fred,
There was a time I'd wish him dead,
A time when I'd see him on the wall,
Sitting frozen, I'd watch him crawl.
Sitting there, my skin would itch,
Watching how his long legs twitched,
He'd crawl upon the bedroom wall,
And to my father I would call.
My dad would come into the room,
And try and squish him with a broom,
Or swat him with a newspaper,
To end his creepy-crawly caper.
One day I decided it was all too much,
And arranged a spider for me to touch,
I couldn't live my life in fear,
Of such a creature it was clear.
I held a Tarantula, a Chile Rose,
Held it right before my nose,
Feeling brave, I didn't flee,
Even raised money for charity.
Now when I see him I do not cry,
We're quite good friends that Fred and I,
See the spider, I call him Fred,
There was a time I'd wish him dead.

Plot 24 Cemetery Lane

On Cemetery Lane, Plot 24,
Up through the earth it finally tore,
Not quite feeling like it did before,
Something was different but it couldn't be sure,
Its body was cold right to the core,
The pain that it felt wasn't there anymore,
Undernourished like a prisoner of war,
On Cemetery Lane, Plot 24.

At Plot 24 Cemetery Lane,
While stumbling through its current domain,
It noticed that it had a craving for brains,
An urge so strong it was hard to contain,
Satiation would be its only gain,
While unsatisfied the desire would remain,
Searching it stumbled on through the rain,
At Plot 24 Cemetery Lane.

At Cemetery Lane's 24th Plot,
Lumbering around like a drunken robot,
Smelling like something left out to rot,
Bleeding from wounds that don't seem to clot,
Maggots are chewing at every raw spot,
It once had a name that it's definitely forgot,
Brought down to the ground by a single gunshot,
At Cemetery Lane's 24th Plot.

You are looking through me but I can see through you,
Like a ghost in the night I see all that you do,
You don't know that I'm here while you go about your day,
I'm invisibly clear and with your mind I will play,
You think you hear someone breathing behind you,
When you look you see nothing but you haven't got a clue,
As I play a few more tricks like moving a pen,
You think you're going mad until you see it again,
You think it's a spirit, a phantom or a ghost,
You never would dream you've an invisible host,
As you snoop round my home bagging my possessions,
I feel that it's time I should teach you a lesson,
I grab your swag off you and push you to the floor,
"Now pick yourself up," I say, "you can leave through that door,"
Still in shock you get up and dust yourself down,
Unbelieving your eyes as your swag floats around,
You came to steal but now you tremble in fear,
Now comes the end of your criminal career,
Because the house that you'd chosen to steel all you can,
Belongs to the one and only Invisible Man.

The Poltergeist Lives In Our House

Malevolent, Destructive,

But sometimes constructive,

The poltergeist lives in our house,

Lights flicker, Bulbs break,

While the bed starts to shake,

The poltergeist lives in our house,

Mischievous, Disruptive,

It's temper eruptive,

The poltergeist lives in our house,

Book fly, Shelves fall,

And plates crash against walls.

The poltergeist lives in our house,

Chairs dance, Door slam,

Some think it's a scam,

That a poltergeist could live in our house.

Vampire

Darkness through the night it crept,
Draped in black and red it swept,
Intense is the hunger,
Can't hold back any longer,
Onto the bed it leapt.

Victim stirs but doesn't awake,
Unknowing just what is at stake,
Fangs sink slowly in,
And the gorging begins,
For the last drop of blood it can take.

Through the window a small hint of light,
Announcing the end of the night,
Just time to escape,
With a flick of its cape,
Changes into a bat and takes flight.

For the victim this was all just a dream,
As the day hears a terrified scream,
Girl found in her bed,
Body limp declared dead,
Heart has stopped in the night it would seem.

☺

CREDITS

My influences for writing these poems.

Starring:

Life – influenced by how out of control everything is during life.

Inside My Teenage Mind – Influenced by mine and other's teenage years.

Mirrored Awareness – Influenced by puberty and all its challenges.

Go Out And Get It – Influenced by being held back as a woman.

Babies Are Not For Me – Influenced by my decision to not have kids.

A Father's Approval – Influenced by a child's struggle to get approval from their father.

A Mother Like No Other – Written for my wonderful mum.

Life Is Just One Big Adventure – Encouragement to throw caution to the wind and enjoy what life has to offer.

The Path Of Pressure – Influenced by the amount of pressure that's thrown upon you as you grow up.

Old Age Comes To Us All – Influenced by how some people treat pensioners.

Optimistic Magpie – Influenced by how optimism rules the heart.

That Smile You Love – Influenced by love and happiness.

Like Eleanor Rigby – Influenced by loneliness and The Beatles Elanor Rigby song.

Windows To The Soul – Brought about by something my dad once said to me about being able to see everything I needed to know in a person eyes.

Breaking Up Is Hard To Do – Influenced by the words spoken during a break up.

Loving You – Influenced by true love.

Smile – Influenced by the song 'Tears of a Clown' and how you smile even though inside you're sad.

Liberation – Influenced by the realisation that you're better off without him even though he split up with you.

Our Future In Racing – Written for old couple that used to race past on their Motobility scooters while I waited for the swimming pool to open.

I'm In Love With A Punk Rock Guitarist – Influenced by a certain punk rock guitarist.

Co-Starring:

Rat Race – Written while in many a traffic jam to and from work.

Money – Influenced by how my money never seems to last.

Poos At Work – My money saving tip.

Writers Block – Influenced by how hard it is to come up with an idea sometimes.

Enough Of It All – How you feel when the shit hits the fan.

Benefit Fraudsters – For the people who claim benefits when they should be out to work....You know who you are...Well you influenced this.

Me And My Clone – On those mornings when I wish I could stay in bed...If only...

Work Life – How time goes fast when you're having fun but at work it drags its worm ridden butt.

If I Won The Lottery – What I would do if this came true.

Boredom – Well, what can I say really, I was bored one day!

A Chocolate Fix – Influenced by my addiction needs.

Wannabe Welly Wearers – By people who go to festivals to be hip but have no real idea what they are about.

Expiration From Smoke Inhalation – Influenced by the disgusting habit that is smoking.

Fad Diet Bimbo – Influenced by the skinny bimbo who complains that she is fat.

Possessions – Influenced by people who can't live life without having everything.

Three Thirty-Three In The Morning – That early morning wee that you don't want to get out of bed for.

You Booze You Lose – Influenced by those who don't know when to stop.

Procrastination – How easily it is to get distracted rather than do what you're supposed to.

The Battle of The Bulges – My constant struggle to lose weight.

Sweet Cravings – My reason for not being able to lose weight...my sweet tooth.

News Today (Distraction Of The Blind) – How important news gets covered up by something trivial in our newspapers.

Haribo Gangster – About young gang crime.

With Special Appearance From:

Global Disaster – Influenced by the song 'Big Yellow Taxi' and how we are building things all over the countryside. Written to the tune of 'A Few Of My Favourite Things.'

Terrorist On Terrafirma – Influenced by the 9/11 and 7/7 terrorist acts and how terrorists are hiding under right our noses because we let them in.

Brainwashed Heroes – About how glamorised war used to be.

Times They Are A Changing – About going into the computer age and how its changed things we do.

DJ Dictators – Influenced by XFactor and how they play the same things over and over on the radio.

Parliament's Infinite Wisdom – How Parliament always seems to make the wrong decisions. Influenced by the riots of 2011.

Mother Nature – Influenced by how we destroy the natural world and how Mother Nature gets her own back with storms etc.

Christmas Comes Earlier Each Year – Influenced by how early Christmas is brought about in the shops.

Halloween – Written about my favourite time of the year.

Hammer Horror Rules – An ode to my favourite movie production company and its actors.

My Life As A So Called Ghost – Influenced by how you can go around every day and no one notices your there.

Dreams Of Pigs With Angels Wings – Influenced by nightmares and how weird and scary they can be.

Werewolf – One of my favourite horror film scares that used to give me nightmares.

The Spider Called Fred – Influenced by my spider hold for charity gratefully organised by the **Exotic Pet Refuge in Deeping St James, Lincolnshire** who do such a brilliant job of looking after people's unwanted exotic pets.

Plot 24 Cemetery Lane – Influenced by another horror film favourite, the Zombie.

The Invisible Man – Written after reading HG Wells, The Invisible Man. Now you know why the title is missing, it's actually there but you just can't see it.

The Poltergeist Lives In Our House – Influenced by ghosts who make their presence known.

Vampire – Another horror favourite.

☺

Bonus Poems

This is for the stay-fast people who sit through the credits of the movie in case there is an extra bit at the end. The people never leave football before the final whistle even when their team is losing and all hope seems to be lost. These people are the believers and it is because of you that I have hidden some poems at the end of the book. I believe people who never give up should be rewarded.

For the stay-fast believers and the people who bought my first edition, here are FOUR extra poems for your enjoyment. Read on for your rewards.

You're Mine

You're my rainbow when it's raining,
You're my sunshine when it's grey,
You're the stars that light up night sky,
Until the moon comes out to play.
You're my world that keeps on turning,
You're the rain that helps things grow,
You're the man I've always dreamed off,
And I just want you to know,
I love you deep with all my heart,
And I'll love you for all time,
And I'll always be happy and smiling,
Just knowing that you're mine.

Online Date Cheat

You claim that you are single,
You're alone in your life,
But the real story is,
Two kids, a dog and a wife.

You log in every day,
To talk to single girls,
It's becoming an addiction,
Taking over your world.

Do you think of your family,
While you flirt with girls online,
Do their feelings come into it,
Or are they forgotten for that time.

Your wife thinks you love her,
She'd trust you to the end,
Can't you see that you're hurting her,
With the emails you will send.

You keep your options open,
Always looking for more,
Never knowing what you've got,
'Til it's walking out the door.

You live for the online buzz,
Of young girls praising you,
Believing that they're single,
But they're married just like you.

Seems like vows count for nothing,
Love's security a farce,
Commitment is a joke to you,
You two-timing arse.

Time

How is it that time seems to know,
When you're having fun it just seems to go,
Holidays they go fast,
And are soon in the past,
Leaving you back at work feeling low.

At work time never goes quick,
To the point when you're just feeling sick,
You dream of the day,
No work and all play,
Until then you'll just watch the clock tick

Our Nan

Roses bloom then fade away,

But always in our memories stay,

Those special times we took for granted,

The lessons, just like seeds, you planted,

While growing up you were always to hand,

That special person we called our Nan.

www.ingramcontent.com/pod-product-compliance
Lightning Source LLC
Chambersburg PA
CBHW061005050726
47592CB00003B/1350

* 9 7 8 0 9 5 7 4 5 3 7 3 9 *